T0064561

In This Moment

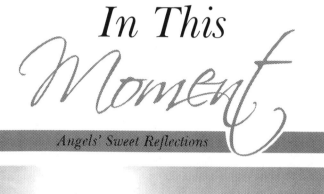

Angels' Sweet Reflections

BRENDA RACHEL

BALBOA PRESS

A DIVISION OF HAY HOUSE

Copyright © 2015 Brenda Rachel.

All rights reserved. No part of this book may be used or reproduced by any means, graphic, electronic, or mechanical, including photocopying, recording, taping or by any information storage retrieval system without the written permission of the author except in the case of brief quotations embodied in critical articles and reviews.

Balboa Press books may be ordered through booksellers or by contacting:

Balboa Press
A Division of Hay House
1663 Liberty Drive
Bloomington, IN 47403
www.balboapress.com
1 (877) 407-4847

Because of the dynamic nature of the Internet, any web addresses or links contained in this book may have changed since publication and may no longer be valid. The views expressed in this work are solely those of the author and do not necessarily reflect the views of the publisher, and the publisher hereby disclaims any responsibility for them.

The author of this book does not dispense medical advice or prescribe the use of any technique as a form of treatment for physical, emotional, or medical problems without the advice of a physician, either directly or indirectly. The intent of the author is only to offer information of a general nature to help you in your quest for emotional and spiritual well-being. In the event you use any of the information in this book for yourself, which is your constitutional right, the author and the publisher assume no responsibility for your actions.

Any people depicted in stock imagery provided by Thinkstock are models, and such images are being used for illustrative purposes only. Certain stock imagery © Thinkstock.

Print information available on the last page.

ISBN: 978-1-5043-3537-9 (sc)
ISBN: 978-1-5043-3536-2 (e)

Balboa Press rev. date: 08/25/2015

CONTENTS

My Sweet Reflections

LOVE

We Heal With Our Minds. We Love With Our Hearts. We can Bring Love to All Mankind. We are the One Wherein It Starts.

Love Heals. Being in Love is Healing. When We are Loved, We can be Healed. To Show Unconditional Love is the Greatest Healer of All.

Love is All-Weather, Not Just All-Seasonal. Love Will Carry Us Through any Snow Storm, Rain Storm, Wind Storm or Sand Storm, but Especially Through any Heart-Storm.

My Sweet Reflections

Love Will Ignite an Eternal Light When We Stop the Fight and Make Our World Right

Simplicity is the Pattern used to Shape our Cloak of Understanding, by Weaving Threads of Love, Honesty and Trust into the Fabric of our Life

When We Close the Door on Our Heart to Love, the Window to Our Soul is Pained

Love is the Most Powerful Energy Available to Us. Love can Heal a Broken Heart, Give Our Life's Purpose a Kick-Start, Have Negativity Depart and Allow Empowerment to Re-Start.

My Sweet Reflections

We can All be Ambassadors of Love (A.O.L.). There is No Monetary Remuneration. Benefits are Unlimited. Rewards are Limitless. All Applicants are Accepted.

Passion is "PASS I(T) ON" without the "T". Living Our Passion Enables Us to Pass "IT" (Kindness, Love, Compassion) On to Each Other.

In the Absence of Love, There is Fear. Love is Fear *"In Absentia"*.

When We can Live as One, We Will All Get Along, Darkness Will be Gone, Hatred Will be Done and Love Will Heal Everyone

My Sweet Reflections

When Our Hearts are Closed, Fear is Exposed. Where Love is Shone, Fear is Gone.

Having Harmony in Our Hearts is Orchestrated by the Instrumentation of Inspiration, Composed by Connecting Chords with the Lyrics of Love

We are Here To Experience and Be Expressions of Love. May Your Heart be Filled with Love Today.

Love is Infinite. Infinite is All-Encompassing. Infinity is Endless Time and Space. May Our Infinite Love Permeate Through Infinity.

My Sweet Reflections

Release Fear. Receive Love.

When Our Anger Becomes Rage, Leading to Danger, We can Ask the "Love" Ranger to Ride his "Trusting" Steed into Our Hearts, Setting Off a "Light" Explosion, Exploding the "Darkness", Leaving Only Peace in His Stead

Do To Another As You Would Want Done To You. Be To Another How You Would Want Another To Be. Love Another In The Way You Would Want To Be Loved.

Love Heals. Loss Steals. Listening Reveals.

My Sweet Reflections

May Our Hearts be Filled with Joy and Love as We Express Our Gratitude Today

Be Love. See Love. Live Free with Love.

Have You Ever Wondered why the Words "Life", "Like", "Live" and "Love" Start with "L" and end in "E"? These are Liberating Expressions. Love Life How You Like to Live. Live Life How You Like to Love.

The Circle of Love has No Beginning and No End. Everyone is Welcome. We Invite You to Join Our Circle of Love Today.

My Sweet Reflections

If We Take a Chance on Opening Our Heart to Love, this Will Give Love a Chance to Find an Opening to Our Heart

When We Feel Unloved and Unlovable, there is a Hole in Our Soul. When We Allow Ourselves to Accept and Receive Love, Our Soul is Whole.

My Sweet Reflections

PEACE

Healing Prayer: Let Us Show Love Where There is None. Bring Light Where None has Shone. Be Kind When Hope has Gone. Live in Peace with Everyone.

When We are at Peace Within Ourselves, the Outer Conflict has been Resolved with the Inner Struggle and We are No Longer Conflicted or Struggling

World Peace is Sought. Living in Peace is Taught. Being at Peace Starts with Thought.

My Sweet Reflections

May Peace and Joy Be Yours Today!

May All Hearts be at Peace. May All Minds be at Rest. May All Conflicts be Ceased, so One World Will Exist.

Let Our "Lights of Love" Shine Through Our Spirits, so that a Universal "Transformation of Peace" can Transition Throughout Our World

May We All Find Peace, Love and Joy. May Our World's Heart Be at Peace.

When We Have Inner Peace Our Negative Thoughts Cease, Positive Energy is Released and Personal Power is Increased

My Sweet Reflections

Our Light Shining from the Inside Reflects Our Living Peacefully on the Outside

When We Totally Understand the Truth that: Living Peacefully Together Exists, Only When We have a Total Understanding of Peace

Through Forgiveness We Release. By Forgiving We Find Peace.

My Sweet Reflections

HOPE

Every Step, Every Breath is the Start of
a New Beginning

In Searching for the Meaning of Life, it
is Possible to Find that Life has Meaning

We can Be a Part of Helping Others
to Heal, Be Healed Ourselves and Be
a Part of the Whole in Healing Our
Planet

For it is in Giving We Receive, it is in
Forgiving We Release

My Sweet Reflections

Through Change We Grow. Through Growth We Change.

While We are Not Able to Fully Understand Another Person's Pain, We are Fully Capable of Understanding a Person in Pain

"Can Do It" is the Conduit that Enables Us to Believe "WE CAN DO IT"

Making Changes in Our Life Can Be Life Changing

When We Have an Opportunity to Lift Up Another Person, We, Ourselves, are Uplifted

My Sweet Reflections

Whatever We Fear We Can Choose to Embrace. Whatever We Embrace We Can Choose Not to Fear.

In Letting Go, We Get to Live

Building Self-Confidence is like Building a Sand Castle - One Grain at a Time

Today I will be Taught. Tomorrow I will Teach. I Can Change My Thoughts to Formulate New Speech.

If We Find We are Imprisoning Ourselves with the Chains of Negative Thought, We are the Only Ones Who Hold the Key to Unlocking these Chains and Securing Our Freedom

My Sweet Reflections

JOY

Love Joyously so We can Forgive with Joy and Live Joyfully

Enjoy Each Moment, for it is in this Pure Enjoyment We Experience the Purest Joy

Share Your Smile Today. It May Heal a Heart.

There are Two Kinds of Attitude: "Long"itude and "Laugh"titude. May Your World Intersect at Laughter and Joy Today!

My Sweet Reflections

When We Shine Our Inner Light, the World Becomes a Brighter Place. Let Our Light Shine Today.

There is as Much Joy in Giving as there is in Giving with Joy

When We Share Joy in Our World, Our Hearts are Warm. Let There Be Joy on Earth.

Sending a Smile Your Way Today. Pass It On!

Joy to Our World. May Our Love Shine So We Can Live As One.

My Sweet Reflections

Each Moment is an Opportunity for Us to Reach Our Optimum Momentum for Maximum Enjoyment

Enjoy the Journey "In Joy"

The Radiance of Our Inner Beauty Reflects Outwardly Through Our Radiant Light

We Feel Fulfilled when We Live a Rich Full Life by Living in the Fulfillment of Peace, Love and Joy

Live Life Harmoniously. Love Life Passionately. Live Love Joyfully.

My Sweet Reflections

Enjoyment Comes from Living with Joy
in the Moment

Have a Wonderfully Joyful Day Filled
with Joy and Wonder

My Sweet Reflections

ENCOURAGEMENT

Make a Difference To Someone, Rather Than Make Fun of a Difference In Someone

We can All Be Winners of the Humanitarian Lifetime Achievement Award for Our Supporting Role in "Providing Support and Being Supportive"

Live Life Purposefully in Order to Enjoy a Purpose-Filled Life

My Sweet Reflections

If We Have Ever Felt Disempowered by Another Person's Actions and/or Words, it is When We Take Our Power Back that We Become Powerful

As a "Lighthouse" Does, We can Shine our Beacon of Light upon Anyone in Distress, Offering Them Comfort, Safety and Warmth

It May Cost Something to Connect To Someone, but it is Absolutely Free to Connect With Someone

Dream the Dream. Envision the Vision. Intend the Intention. Materialize the Manifestation. Embrace the Experience.

My Sweet Reflections

In Letting Go, We are Free. It is Freeing to Let Go.

To Eradicate Feelings of Unworthiness and Worthlessness, We Must Believe that We are Worthy of Self-Worth, in Order to Embrace Our Worth and Accept Our Worthiness

When We Feel Conquered by Fear, We can Choose to Conquer Our "Thoughts of Mass Destruction" by Surrendering to "The Light", Knowing that this is Our Greatest Conquest

My Sweet Reflections

Plant the Seed. Stand Firmly on the Ground. Till the Soil. Watch the Idea Grow Round and Round. Reap the Harvest. The Fruits of Our Labour are Found.

When We Treat Each Other Respectfully with Respect, Our Treat is the Reward of More Respectful Self-Respect

We are Given the Gift of Sight When We Recognize the Insight that is Awarded to Us through Our Foresight

We are Able to Empower Others When We, Ourselves, are Empowered, by Combining Our Empathy with Our Own Power

My Sweet Reflections

Greatness can Be Achieved by Doing Small Things Great

The Past has Shaped Us into Who We Are Today. From This Moment Forward, We can Mold Ourselves into Who We Want To Be.

When We Keep Our Thoughts in a State of Ascension Rather than Dissension, Our Positive Intentions Become Wonderful Manifestations

It is Worth Knowing that One of the Hardest Lessons in Life to Learn can be Knowing Our Own Worth, and that We are Worthy of Being Known

My Sweet Reflections

When We Seek Help, It is in Helping Others We May Find that We are Being Helped

There are People with No Hearing Who are Willing Listeners. There are People with Hearing Who are Unwilling to Listen. We can Make a Choice to Listen to Someone Today.

The Confirmation of Our Intention is Affirmed through the Intent of Our Affirmation

My Sweet Reflections

We can be Our Own Oppressors by Repressing Our Thoughts Through Limiting Beliefs, Causing the Suppression of Our Advancement in Life

If We Could Let Go of Creating Drama, We Would Experience Less Trauma and Our Lives Would be Much Calmer

Life can be Compared to Performing on a Balance Beam. By Staying Calm, Focused and Trusting in Our Ability, We can Overcome the Difficult Positions We Find Ourselves In.

Can One Person Make a Difference? Yes! That Person Can Be You Today!

My Sweet Reflections

Appreciation is One of the Nicest Expressions of Gratitude We Can be Shown, as it Confirms and Validates Our Value by Being Appreciated

When I can See the Beauty in You and You can See the Beauty in Me, Together We are Beautiful

To Ascend to the Peak of Our Mountain of "I Achieve What I Believe" We Need Tenacity, Voracity and Elasticity

Thank You for Your Caring By Sharing

My Sweet Reflections

Some of the Strongest People on the Outside are the Weakest and Most Vulnerable on the Inside. If You Sense Someone Needs a Kind Word, They Probably Do.

When We are at the End of Our Endurance of Whatever We are Having to Endure, Remember to Say Something Endearing to Ourselves, to Encourage Ourselves to Stay Strong, for the Remainder of Whatever it is We Have to Endure

Please Be Wise. Words Can Be Sharp as Knives, Even in Disguise. People End Their Lives by Being Criticized and Demoralized.

My Sweet Reflections

While Grief is a "Solo Journey", We can Provide Comfort and Support to Those Souls Who are Grief-Stricken

When We are Connected to Our "Power Source", a Current of Radiant "Light" Energy Surges Through Us for All to See

Sometimes it Takes Courage to Say We are Wrong, Especially When We are the Ones Who have been Wronged. When We Forgive the Wrongdoer, Our Courageousness Shines Through.

Live Life with Purpose to Fulfill your Purpose in Life

My Sweet Reflections

Kindness - Listed on the Communal Life Exchange - Public Offering States "Open to All, Unlimited Growth Potential, Value - a One to One Share".

Each of Us can Encourage Someone Who is Discouraged by Helping Them to Find Their Inner Courage

We Have Heard the Quote "Beauty is in the Eyes of The Beholder". Today I Encourage You to "Behold Your Inner Beauty" and See Yourself as the "Beautiful Human Being You Are".

My Sweet Reflections

As We Become Stronger in Validating Our Sense of Worthiness, We can Begin to Invalidate Our Feelings of Worthlessness

We can be Supportive by Offering Support to Those Who Need to be Supported

We Must Believe the Belief that, "We are Able to Be, Do or Have Anything We are Striving to Achieve". Through Our Belief, We Achieve.

My Sweet Reflections

Compassion is When We Combine "Comforting with Passion" to Embrace Others Who Need to be Comforted from Their Dispassion

When We are Living Our Passion Our Faces Glow, Our Hearts are Whole and there is a Fire Burning in Our Soul

My Sweet Reflections

SPIRITUAL

The Four Faces of Love: GOD is LOVE, I AM LOVE, YOU are LOVE, WE are LOVE. LOVE IS ALL THERE IS.

Angels' Spiritual Service Centre: Offering a Free Reality Check, which includes: an Attitude Adjustment to Change Thoughts, Boosting Energy Levels, Leading to Excellent Performance, Creating Optimum Power

Being Lighthearted around Those Who are Disheartened Manifests in a Heartfelt Heart-to-Heart Human Connection

My Sweet Reflections

When We are in Our Darkest Hour, Feeling We Have Lost Our Power, Turn to "The Light" and Ask for "Sight" to Heal Our Heavy Heart, Giving Us a Fresh Start

There are Many Measures We Take that Lead Us on the Road to Success. When We Take the "High Road" We Achieve Immeasurable Success.

When We Accept the Imperfections of Our Human "Beingness", We can Embrace the Perfection of Our Spiritual "Being", Knowing We Came Here Complete, Perfect and Whole

My Sweet Reflections

May We See the Grace of God in Each Other, So We May Feel the Graciousness of God Together

Kindness is a Virtue. Being Kind to Each Other Allows Us to Live Virtuously.

To Create a Creation that Originates from our Creator is the Most Wonderful Way to Express Our Creative Expression

"Grateful" Reminders are a Great Way to be Reminded of What We are Grateful For

My Sweet Reflections

An "Eclipse of the Heart" Occurs when God's Light Covers any Darkness which Encircles our Heart. May God's Light Surround Our Hearts Today.

When Our Bodies are Broken and Our Hearts are Hurt, We Thank God in Heaven for Healing Us on Earth

God's Masterpiece entitled "The Perfection of Humanity" is now being displayed in "Harmony Hall". This Brilliant Mosaic is formed by the Connection of Individual "Diamonds" Sparkling from the Brilliance of their "Light" and "Love".

My Sweet Reflections

When We Embark on Our "Solo" Journey, We may Experience Turbulent Thoughts, Unexpected Delays, a Change in Direction and/or a Decline in Altitude. Once Transcended, We Find Clarity to Reach Our Destination to a Calm and Peaceful "Journey of the Soul".

When We are in Need of Protecting Ourselves from any Inner or Outer Conflict, Remember to Ask the Angels for "Divine Protection" and We Will Immediately be Protected

We Can Choose to Listen to Our Inner Voice: "Make Things Right, So Others Will See Our Outer Light

My Sweet Reflections

If a Wise Man Were to Say, "I Sit, I Stare, I See Beauty Everywhere". Could it Mean, "Being Still in the Silence is Beautiful, While Feeling the Beauty of the Silence in the Stillness"?

May We See the Face of God's Grace Throughout the Human Race

When Our Soul is Aflame and Burning Bright, Our Hearts Begin to Glow with Inner Light, Our Passion Comes Alive, Our Visions Start to Thrive, We Know that, for Today, Our Life is Right

Kindness is an Expression of God's Love. Expressing God's Love is Kindness.

My Sweet Reflections

As We Become More and More Visible Sharing Our God-Given Gifts, We Realize that the Real Gift to Us is that Our Invisibility has Become Visible

There is No Value in Being "Right" just so We can Be "Righteous". There is Unlimited Value in Living in "Rightness".

Meditation is the Angels' Invitation to Us for Contemplation

Tri-Lights Shine Their Light on Three Settings: Bright, Brighter, and Brightest. Similarly; We can Shine Our Tri-Lights of Love, Joy and Happiness to Make Our World the Brightest Place.

My Sweet Reflections

When our Confidence has been Shattered and Our Hearts have been Battered, We Know that God's Love is All that Matters

In the Stillness of God's Presence, We Can Be Present

Before We Can Trust Another Wholeheartedly, We Must Wholly Trust Our Heart

When We are Electrically Charged by Connecting to Our "Power Source", We have Unlimited Energy and can be Continually Recharged to Energize Those Who Connect With Us

My Sweet Reflections

As We Face Our Challenges Head On, and Frustration Comes Along, Do Not Throw Our Hands Up in the Air, but Turn to Our Hearts and Say a Silent Prayer

When We are Intuitively Guided to be Expressions for God, We are Reflections of God Expressing Through Us

Divine Love is Our Birthright. It is Universal Music. We can All be the Instruments to Channel this Beautiful Angelic Music.

When We Stand in Our Truth, No Matter How Many Deviations, Detractions or Distractions We Make or Take, We Will Always End "Up Right", Upright

My Sweet Reflections

"Hallucination" can be Hearing or Seeing Things that are Not Present. "Hallelucination" is the Joyful Affirming of God's Presence, While We Accept and Receive God's Presents.

By Silencing Our Minds, We Can Be Still in the Silence, Knowing We are Blessed by Being Silent

Recognition: When I Look at You and You Look At Me and We See Each Other.

Reflection: When You and I Look at Each Other and We See Ourselves in Each Other.

Realization: When You and I Look at Each Other and We See Our Oneness.

My Sweet Reflections

When We Feel All Alone and that We Have to "Do It" on Our Own, We can Choose to Make a Choice, to Listen to Our Inner Voice, Kneeling Down in Prayer, Knowing God is There

May We Be Caring and Compassionate with Each Other so that Our Spirits Become Connected

Strength Results from the Gentleness of Our Spirit Resonating with Our Gentle Soul

Remember When We Count Our Blessings One by One that We are a Blessing from the "One"

My Sweet Reflections

Find Calm in the Midst of Chaos by Remembering that in Each Moment, Every Breath We Take is a Gift from God. Be Grateful For This Gift.

Imagine You are Staring at Yourself through an Imaginary Looking Glass. Can You Tell the Image You See "I am Beautiful, I Love Me Just The Way I Am Today"? See Yourself Beautiful. God Does!

Being of Service to Others is One of the Most Rewarding Ways to Serve God. Our Serving is Our Reward.

My Sweet Reflections

Divine Love is the Gift God Bestowed upon Us from Birth. May Our Love Divinely Shine Through to Everyone Today.

Dear God: Please Ease the Pain from My Anger so Relief is Felt in My Heart

"Spiritsizing" Classes are Offered to Strengthen Our Relationship with Spirit. We Can Use the "Faithcycle" which Allows Us to Live the Cycle of Our Life in the Momentum of Faith; the "Trustmill" which Allows Our Thoughts to Constantly Revolve Around Trust; and the "Love Balance Beam" which Keeps Us Balanced in Peace and Harmony by Standing Firm in Our Love for Ourselves and Others.

My Sweet Reflections

Those Who Believe in "The Divine" Know that Everything is Divinely Orchestrated

Divine Intervention is the Angels' Way of Intervening so We are Protected and Will Remain on Our Divine Path

Spiritual Congruency Occurs When Our Thoughts Align Congruently with Our Actions in a Positive Manner

Bless Others, Even When We Feel Our Blessings are Absent. It is in Blessing Others that We are Truly Blessed.

Shine Our Lights So We Can Guide Someone Who is in Darkness "Home"

My Sweet Reflections

Affirmation for Deservedness: This is My Time to Shine. Everything I Deserve is Rightly Mine. All Things Come From "The Divine".

When We Experience the Loss of a Loved One, there is a "Hole in Our Soul". Remember to Turn to the "Holy One" to Ask for Wholeness.

The "Universal Banquet Hall" is Open to Everyone. Please Choose from the Following Menu Items: "Joy Juice", "Love Libations", "Faith-Filled Filets", "Harmony Hearts", "Satisfied Sole", "Grapes of Gratitude", "Kindness Kisses", "Trust Treats", and "Peace Pie". Enjoy!

My Sweet Reflections

Our Angels are Close at Hand, to Help Us to Take a Stand, to Feel Alive, to Be Revived, to Let Go of Worry, to Slow Down – Not Hurry, to Keep Us from Harm, to Stay Safe and Warm, to Surround Us with Love, from God Above

When We Feel Tired, Have No Desire, Are Not Inspired, Ask God to Rekindle Our "Inner Fire"

From the Sanctum of Our Inner Soul, Where We Know We Came Here Whole, We Hold Memories of Perfect Bliss, Knowing We are Completely Blessed

My Sweet Reflections

When We Feel Misunderstood, God Understands. When We Feel Unheard, God Hears. When We Feel Unseen, God Sees. When We Feel Unloved, God Loves, US.

Welcome to God's (G.O.L.F.) God Offers Love Freely Course. Connect with the "Trust" Tee, Take a "Solid Stance", Focus on the "Fair Way" to Align with the "Whole" in One's Soul.

Enlightenment Perpetuates Enrichment, which Propels Enhancement, which Promotes Enthusiasm, which Produces Enjoyment

My Sweet Reflections

A Soul is Never Lost, Only Veered off the Pathway of the Goodness of Life, Waiting to be Found, Wanting to be Saved

Minds are Powerful. Prayers are Healing. Through Mindful Prayer We can Receive a Powerful Healing.

Caring Opens Our Minds. Compassion Opens Our Hearts. Connection Opens Our Spirits.

Believing Our Life is Wonderful Gives Us the Opportunity to Live Our Lives Full of Wonder

My Sweet Reflections

Gratitude is Being Grateful with "Attitude"

When We Find Ourselves in Distress Emotionally, Physically and/or Spiritually, this is a Good Time to "De-Stress"

When We Give From the Heart, We are Givers with Heart

For Every Soul there is a "Soulution"

Many of Us have Heard the Phrase "Wonders Never Cease." I Believe it is Important to Never Cease Our Wonder of All the Blessings We have Received.

My Sweet Reflections

When We Allow Outside Circumstances to Usurp Our Inner Power, We May Feel Powerless. When We Turn to Our "Higher Power" We Become Empowered.

The Truth about Trust is that, Before We Can Truly Trust Someone Else, We Must First Trust Ourselves

When We Laugh, Our Eyes are Bright, Our Hearts are Light and Our Soul is Right

In the Quiet and Solitude "Soul"itude is Found

My Sweet Reflections

UNIVERSAL MESSAGES

One Heart. One Mind. One World.

Truth and Trust are Necessary to the Transformation of Our Global Consciousness

Being Kind to Others is One of the Kindest Things We can Do For Ourselves, as Kindness Promotes "Kinship"

My Sweet Reflections

Great Leaders Have a Responsible Role to Provide Good Leadership by Leading by Example, Guided by Their Unwavering Moral Compass, Necessary to Empower and Inspire the Morale of Others

Chance Encounters Give Us the Chance for Encountering New Opportunities

If We React Negatively, then it is Unlikely the Response Will be Positive. If We Respond Positively, then it is Unlikely the Reaction Will be Negative.

My Sweet Reflections

It is Possible for Us to Change Our Thoughts from We Have "Limited Possibilities" to Thoughts of "It is Possible to Have Unlimited Possibilities"

Our Challenge Today is to Challenge the Challenge

When We Focus Our Attention on Dreams of Long Ago, We Deter Ourselves from Focusing on Our Vision for Today

Changing Direction Directs Change

My Sweet Reflections

Most of Us Can Say that We are Not Perfect. By Embracing Our Imperfectness and Accepting Our Imperfections, We Come to an Understanding of Perfection.

If We Believe We Have Reached Our Greatest Potential, this May Deter Us from Potentially Reaching Our Greatness

When We Trust Ourselves Enough to be Truthful with Others, Transformation Occurs

Gentleness May, at Times, be Seen as Weakness. Sometimes, it Takes Great Strength to be Gentle.

My Sweet Reflections

It is Nice to be Concise, When We Say
We are Contrite, for "Making You Lose"
so "We Can Be Right"

The Changes We Make are from the
Choices We Have Made

We Always Have an Opportunity to
Change "Our Perception" of "The
Perception" to Allow for a "New
Perception"

Believe the Idea. Conceive the Concept.
Receive the Knowledge. Achieve the
Reward.

My Sweet Reflections

Cherish Every Moment, Each Person, All Things; for at a Time Unknown to Us, They Will all Perish

Let Us Not Have Others' Voices Impede Our Choices

Freedom of Expression is Inherent to the Emancipation of Our Spirits, so that We May All "Live Free"

While We are Processing Our Life's Process, We Become "Food for Thought" Processors

My Sweet Reflections

We are Continuously Progressing in Forward Movement. As We Move Forward in Our Life, We See the Continuity of Our Progress.

Before We Can Be of Value to Others, We Must First See the Value in Ourselves

Dreams Inspire Us to Believe. Through Goals We Aspire to Achieve Our Dreams. Our Manifestations Realize Our Dreams and Goals.

When We Unexpectedly Have to Change Directions in Our Life, We Can Direct Our Thoughts to Those of Expectancy

My Sweet Reflections

We May Still be Searching for Our Life's Purpose, but If We are Living a Purposeful Life, We are Fulfilling Our Purpose in Life

Most of Us Believed at One Time or Another We had No Options. At Any Given Moment in Time, We Can Opt In or Opt Out of Optimizing Our Decision-Making Option.

Generosity is a Virtue Attributed to Those Who are Generous by Giving of Themselves Generously

Freedom has No Barriers, Borders or Boundaries

My Sweet Reflections

Thought-Provoking is the Result of the Provocation of Our Thoughts

Sometimes When We Lose Someone, We Find Ourselves. The Reverse is Also True. Sometimes We Lose Ourselves When We Find Someone.

We Live in Changing Times. Perhaps Now is a Good Time for Us to Make Changes in Our Lives.

When We Connect With Someone, It Is In Our Connection That We Feel Connected

My Sweet Reflections

If We Have Ever Felt We Missed an Opportunity to Take a Chance, Chances are, this was Not the Time

When Gladness Replaces Sadness, Happiness Relieves the Madness

Positive Change Results from Negative Thoughts Being Re-Arranged

When We are in an "Indecisive" Period, We are Going Through an "In Decision" Process

When We Engage in Another Person's Negative Drama, We Become Dis-engaged from the Positive Engagement of Our Own Story

My Sweet Reflections

Are We Performing at Our Optimum Capacity or is there Room for Additional Optimal Growth Potential?

Climbing up Our "Ladders of Success" Should Begin with a "Solid Foundation" that Supports Us in Feeling Secure in Our Position, as We Take Our Next Steps

Being Unaware is Unknowing. Being Aware is Knowing. Having Awareness is Knowledge. Once We Know, We Always Know.

When We Choose Goodness over Greatness, it is for Our Greater Good

My Sweet Reflections

As We Continue to Better Ourselves for the Betterment of Our Life, this Helps to Continually Make the World a Better Place

When We Reach Out to Someone Who is Unreachable, It Gives Us the Opportunity to Teach Them, as Long as They are Teachable

Each Day is a New Opportunity for Us to Be Different, See Things Differently, and Do Something to Make a Difference

When We Live with the Attitude of "Need to be Right", We May Lose Sight of What is Actually Right

My Sweet Reflections

Friendship Defines "Friends" Who are "Hip" to Each Other's Needs and Desires

Sometimes We are Challenged. Sometimes We are the Challenger. Sometimes We are Challenging. Sometimes We are Made Stronger by Our Challenges.

We Become Wise, When We Open Our Eyes, Ignore What We Know are Lies and, Empower Ourselves to Re-energize

My Sweet Reflections

INSPIRATIONAL ACRONYMS

(**A.N.G.E.L.S.**) – Asking Nothing, Giving Everything, Loving Spirits.

(**C.A.L.M.**) – Consciously Aligning Liveliness (of Mind, Body, Spirit) with Moderation. Today I am Calm in the Midst of Chaos.

(**D.O.U.B.T.S.**) – Delete Obsolete, Unsupportive Beliefs to Transcend Self-Doubt

(**F.A.I.T.H.**) – Fully Accepting Inspirational Truths for Healing

My Sweet Reflections

God's (**G.R.A.C.E.**) – God's Reflection of Adoration, Creating Empathy

(**G.R.A.C.E.**) – Gratitude and Respect for All Creation Everywhere. Let There Be GRACE on Earth.

(**G.S.T.**) – Giving Selflessly and Thoughtfully

(**H.A.P.P.I.N.E.S.S.**) – Hearing Our Angels (Who Are) Providing Positive Inspiration (To Us) Necessary (To) Experience Soulful Satisfaction

(**H.E.A.L.**) – Helping Everyone to Accept Love

My Sweet Reflections

(**H.E.A.L.I.N.G.**) – Helping Everyone to Affirm "Life is Now Good"

(**H.E.R.O.E.S.**) – Helping Everyone Reach Optimum Enlightenment for Self-Realization

(**H.O.P.E.**) – Helping Others by Providing Encouragement

(**H.S.T.**) – Harmonizing Souls Together

(**K.I.S.S.**) – What is a Spiritual Kiss? Kindness Igniting Soulful Satisfaction.

My Sweet Reflections

(**L.I.G.H.T.**) – I am LIGHT. Living In Goodness, Humility and Truth.

(**L.O.V.E.**) – Letting Ourselves be Vulnerably Engaged

(**M.I.R.A.C.L.E.S.**) – Manifestations of Intuitive Requests, Affirming Confirmation of Life's Exceptional Surprises

(**P.E.A.C.E.**) – Positive Engagement with All Creation Everywhere

(**P.S.T.**) – Personalizing Spiritual Truths

My Sweet Reflections

(**R.A.K.I.S.H.**) – Random Acts of Kindness Initiating Spiritual Healing

(**S.I.M.P.L.I.F.Y.**) – Setting In Motion a Plan Limiting Inventory For Yourself

(**T.R.U.S.T.**) – Taking a Risk Under Spiritual Tutelage

(**W.O.R.S.H.I.P.**) – When Our Religions and Spirituality Have Immeasurable Positivity

ABOUT THE AUTHOR

Brenda Rachel became a Certified Angel Therapy® Practitioner with Doreen Virtue in May 2006.

Brenda Rachel is an inspirational/spiritual songwriter. Her EP "In This Moment" was released on December 2, 2014, through MondoTunes and is on iTunes and Amazon.

Brenda Rachel authored this inspirational/spiritual quote book, *In This Moment Angels' Sweet Reflections*, by having the angels channel each quote to her.

Brenda Rachel resides in Vancouver, British Columbia, with her beloved Miniature American Eskimo dog, Kizia.

http://www.brendarachel4angels.com/

https://plus.google.com/+BrendaRachelTeichroeb444/

https://www.facebook.com/brendarachel444

https://www.linkedin.com/in/brendateichroeb

https://twitter.com/BrendaRachel444

Printed in the United States
By Bookmasters